CROSS STITCHING
on LINEN

✕ ✕ ✕

Favourite Flowers

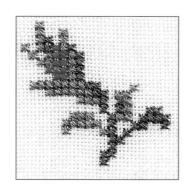

Jane Greenoff

THE
CROSS STITCH
GUILD

Contents

A CROSS STITCH GUILD BOOK
First published in the UK in 2000

Text, designs, photography and layout Copyright © The Cross Stitch Guild 2000
Diagrams Copyright © The Cross Stitch Guild 2000 (diagrams from *The Cross Stitcher's Bible* courtesy of David & Charles
Publishers)
Jane Greenoff has asserted her right to be identified as author of this work in accordance with the Copyright, Designs and
Patents Act, 1988.

ISBN 0-9539085-0-X

Project finishing by Sue Hawkins, Editing by Vivienne Wells, Charts and diagrams by Ethan Danielson,
Photography by Pete Canning, Illustrations by Sarah Jane Gillespie, Book design by Brenda Morrison

Printed in Great Britain by The Amadeus Press Ltd
for The Cross Stitch Guild, Pinks Barn, London Road, Fairford GL7 4AR

Cross Stitching on Linen

I have written this very personal book to remove the myths about stitching on linen and to explain just how simple and rewarding it can be. For those of you who are not convinced, most designs in this book can also be stitched on aida. Where this is not possible, the chart is labelled 'evenweave only'.

What is evenweave?

The fabric used for counted needlework is divided into two main groups: aida, a fabric woven in definite blocks with obvious holes; or evenweave, which is woven in single threads. The evenweave group includes modern linens designed for embroidery (though not all linens are evenweave, see p 7).

The term 'evenweave' refers to the method used to manufacture the fabric; it does not mean that the material will have no lumps and bumps! It means that there is the same number of warp and weft threads in any square of fabric (which is not necessarily the case with ordinary fabrics). So, when you work a cross-stitch on evenweave fabric, the stitch appears square rather than squashed, shortened or elongated. On linen, the fabric threads vary in thickness, so a cross stitch is generally formed over two threads of linen to balance out any variation.

Working over two threads on 28-count evenweave fabric (28 threads to 2.5 cm/1 in) produces the same size stitches as working over a single block on 14-count aida: the stitches are the same size on both fabrics, as is the finished design.

Stitching on linen

Linen, made from fibres of the flax plant (*Linium usitatissimum*) is one of the oldest fabrics. There is evidence in Switzerland of flax working as far back as 8,000BC, and linen cloths were found in the tombs of the Egyptian Pharaohs. When wet, unlike most natural fibres, linen increases in strength and has a high resistance to tearing. (It can absorb up to 120% of its own weight in water, and does not feel damp until it has absorbed 20%). It is the strongest natural fibre, and is recognised by its characteristic coolness, smoothness and sheen – though the irregularity of the individual threads can be seen in even the finest linens.

The strength of linen makes it an ideal fabric for cross stitch, pulled or drawn thread work and Hardanger embroidery: its characteristic creasing ability is an advantage for pulled work, because the threads that are 'pulled' together stay 'pulled', creating the lovely lacy effects of this type of embroidery.

Cashel Linen (28 threads to 2.5 cm/1 in), one of the dozens of evenweave fabrics produced by Zweigart for counted embroidery, is my personal favourite. Many of the designs in this little book are worked on antique white linen, because white produces the best result for the photographs, but if I'm stitching just for myself I love using coloured fabric. The choice of colours available today is extensive, with many beautiful, subtle shades (see the photo on p 5). So, feel free to experiment.

Some days when I am designing or doing the paperwork part of the business I almost have 'withdrawal symptoms' and need to stitch on a lovely new piece of linen. It is so cool and smooth to the touch and handles so well. I even like the smell of the unbleached fabric. I generally prefer to work on linen without washing it first, unless there is a very defined crease which may be difficult to remove later. A new piece of linen may feel a little stiff when you start a project but this will soon disappear with handling.

I can think of nothing better than to settle down with a piece of fine evenweave linen, a good selection of thread and a gold-plated needle. Stitcher's Heaven!

How to work the projects

The following instructions apply to all the designs in this book unless stated otherwise in the project. To help further, I have added tips for perfect cross stitch on linen (p 6–7).

If you use a fabric with a thread count different from the one specified, work out the finished design size and fabric requirements (see p 45). To check a fabric's thread count, lay a ruler on top of it and, using the point of a needle, count the number of threads or blocks to 2.5 cm (1 in).

Check you have all the thread colours you need and mount each colour on a piece of card alongside its shade number.

Preparing the fabric

Centre the design on the fabric and start stitching in the middle of the design to ensure adequate space for finishing (on band samplers, work from one end of the row to the other). To find the middle of the fabric, fold it in four and press lightly. On large projects work a narrow line of tacking (basting) along the folds, following the threads. Remove this when the work is completed.

To prevent fraying, sew a narrow hem round all raw edges, or oversew.

Frames / hoops are not necessary

It is perfectly acceptable to work counted cross stitch and all the projects in this book without a frame or hoop, but, if you must use a hoop, use one large enough to hold the complete design. Moving a hoop across your beautifully formed stitches is such a shame.

Working the cross stitch

With stranded cotton (floss), 80 cm (31.5 in) lengths are perfect for the loop start (you'll get ten lengths per skein). Use shorter lengths of perlé cotton thread as this tends to deteriorate as it is pulled through the fabric.

All cross stitch in this book is worked over two threads of linen using two strands of stranded cotton. Use single strands of perlé.

Use a size 26 needle for all cross stitch, except with perlé thread which needs size 22. For speed and a very neat back, use the loop start (p 58) or refer to 'Perfect Cross Stitch on Linen' (p 6–7). I always work cross stitch in two journeys, using a sewing movement (without a frame) – stitching half each cross stitch on the first journey, then covering those original stitches on the second journey.

This forms single vertical lines on the back which are very neat and give you somewhere to finish the raw ends. The top stitches should all face the same direction.

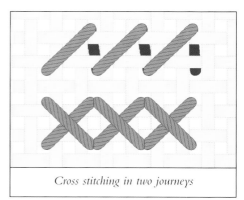

Cross stitching in two journeys

Do not travel across the back of the fabric for more than two stitches, as trailing thread will show through to the front of the work. Plan your route around the chart, counting over short distances to avoid mistakes.

When finishing off, pass the needle under the vertical stitches of the same or similar colour at the back of the work and snip off the loose end close to the stitching. (Small loose ends have a nasty habit of pulling through to the right side.)

Backstitch outlining

Backstitch outlining (optional) is added *after* the cross stitch is complete (p 59). Use one strand of stranded cotton in a slightly smaller size needle. Work over pairs of linen threads, avoiding long stitches.

Perfect Cross Stitch on Linen

To create perfect stitches try the following tips – how seriously you take this advice depends on how much time you have:

- Take two strands of stranded cotton (floss), separate the strands and then realign them before threading your needle. This isn't possible when using the loop start (p 58), in which case experts will be able to see the reversed twist in the threads. It's up to you just how perfectionist you wish to be.
- Start with an away waste knot (p 58). If an away waste knot in a dark thread leaves a faint mark or shadow, this can be removed with a clean toothbrush.
- Pass the threads through a lightly damp sponge to remove unwanted static.
- To check how many strands of stranded cotton (floss) are needed, pull out one thread from the fabric. The thread(s) in your needle should be about the same weight as the fabric thread.
- If you wish to add more detail, work over one thread of the fabric, but complete each stitch as you go, rather than working in two journeys. This prevents the stitches sliding under the fabric threads.

- When you start stitching on linen, begin to the left of a vertical thread. This helps prevent counting mistakes.
- To prevent the threads from 'corkscrewing' slightly, turn the work upside down and allow the needle to drop and spin. Or, better still; learn to twist the needle as you stitch. Each time you take the needle out of the fabric, give the needle a half turn and your stitches will lie flat.
- Avoid coming up through occupied holes (where a stitch has already been formed) from the back. Instead, insert the needle from the front. This prevents spoiling existing perfect stitches.
- Avoid running out of thread halfway across a row or band. If you should do so, 'stitch and park' (see opposite) the short end, start the new thread using an away waste knot (p 58) and work a few stitches, then finish the short end in the direction you are stitching.
- Keep a small, sharp pair of pointed scissors exclusively for your stitching. I use gold plated stork scissors and I wear them around my neck on a ribbon. I also always use gold-plated needles – they make stitching easier and don't mark the fabric.

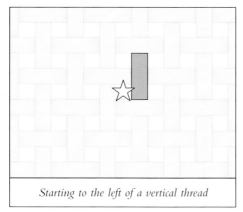

Starting to the left of a vertical thread

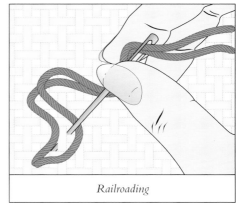

Railroading

Railroading

Railroading is a technique used to force the two strands of stranded cotton (floss) to lie flat and parallel. When pushing the needle through the fabric to make a stitch, pass it in-between the two strands of stranded cotton (floss). You can railroad both parts of the stitch or only the top part. Personally, I find the needle twist method (opposite) has the same effect as railroading and is much quicker.

Stitch and park

When working with a number of different shades you can use several needles to avoid constant threading of the needle. Work a few stitches in one shade, bring the needle out to the front of the work and 'park' it in the fabric above where you are stitching. Introduce another colour; work a few stitches and then park. Bring back the previous colour, working under the back of the stitches in the second colour. Using a gold-plated needle prevents the needle marking the fabric.

Finishing a thread perfectly

Finish the stitches in the direction that you are working. To do this, when the thread needs replacing stop stitching and park the needle above the design. Thread a new needle with the replacement thread and form a few stitches. Now take the first needle and finish the old thread under the new stitches. This prevents any stitch distortion on the front of the work.

Working band samplers

When you have completed one band across the full width of the pattern, sew a line of tacking (basting) stitches from each end of the band of stitches to the top and bottom of the fabric, following the line of the fabric threads carefully. This will save you hours of frustration later on by preventing counting errors. Each band should finish in the same place, exactly in the line of threads marked by the tacking (basting) stitches.

Non-evenweave linen

Non-evenweave linen was used to create samplers and counted masterpieces long before the concept of evenweave had been invented and it can be exciting to attempt to recreate a design on non-evenweave material. You cannot be sure how the design will look when worked on non-evenweave linen, so you need to find out the foibles of your fabric. Always test the fabric by stitching a square of cross stitches: this will show how the shape of the stitches is distorted by the fabric. Then you can position your design on the fabric in a way that minimises the distortion.

What is it worth?

Linen tends to be more expensive than other evenweave fabrics with a mixed content but it will last long after you and I have shuffled off! I feel that when we are planning to spend many hours working a piece of counted embroidery, we should select the most beautiful fabric we can afford. Our time is worth the extra, don't you think?

If you follow the tips for perfect cross stitch, you too can achieve this neatness and consistency

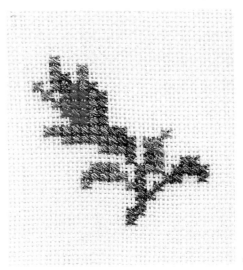

(clockwise from top left)
Rose Band Sampler, Rose & Bow
Pincushion, Rose Scissors Keeper, Rose
Needlecase and Hemstitched Bookmark

Hearts & Roses

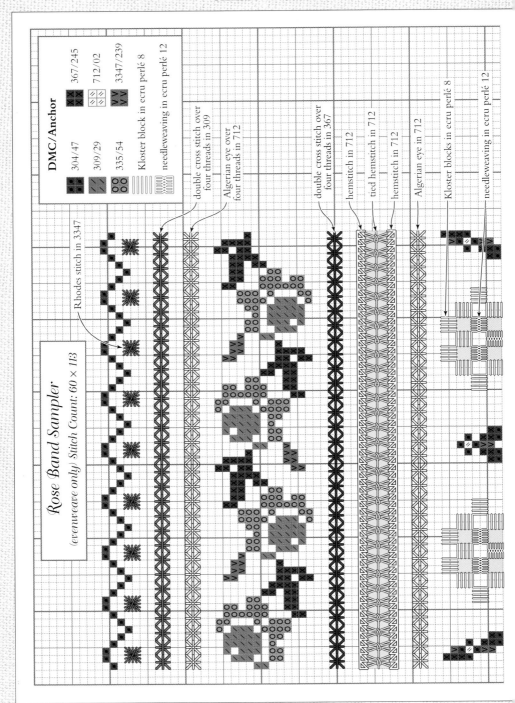

Rose Band Sampler
(evenweave only) Stitch Count: 60 × 113

DMC/Anchor

304/47		367/245	
309/29		712/02	
335/54		3347/239	

Kloster block in ecru perlé 8

needleweaving in ecru perlé 12

Rhodes stitch in 3347

double cross stitch over four threads in 309

Algerian eye over four threads in 712

double cross stitch over four threads in 367

hemstitch in 712

tied hemstitch in 712

hemstitch in 712

Algerian eye in 712

Kloster blocks in ecru perlé 8

needleweaving in ecru perlé 12

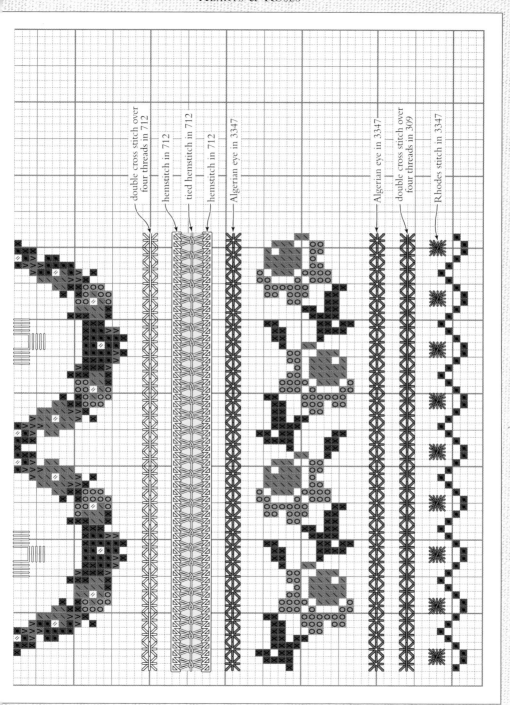

double cross stitch over four threads in 712

hemstitch in 712

tied hemstitch in 712

hemstitch in 712

Algerian eye in 3347

Algerian eye in 3347

double cross stitch over four threads in 309

Rhodes stitch in 3347

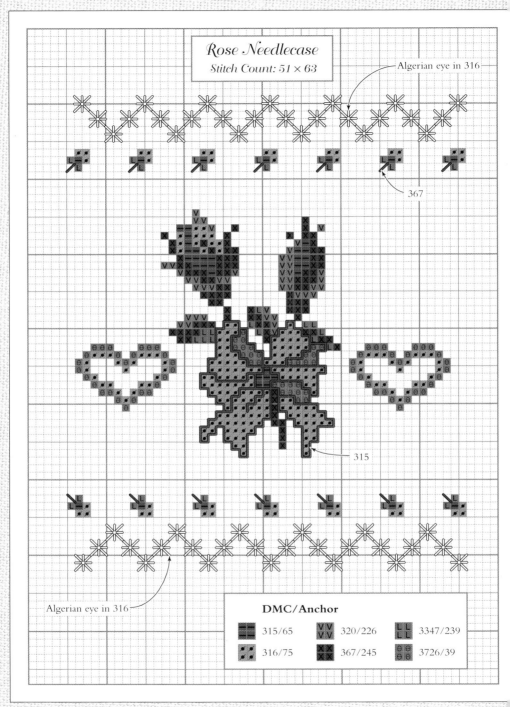

Rose Needlecase
Stitch Count: 51 × 63

Algerian eye in 316

367

315

Algerian eye in 316

DMC/Anchor

▦ 315/65	V V / V V	320/226	L L / L L	3347/239
316/75	X X / X X	367/245	θ θ / θ θ	3726/39

12

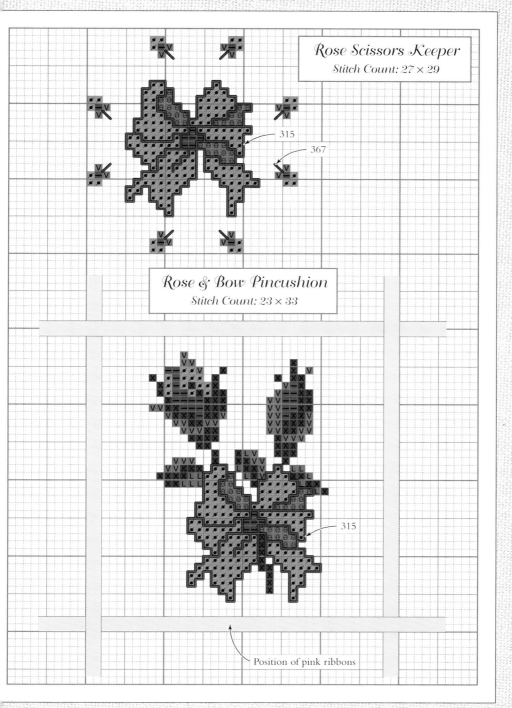

Rose Scissors Keeper
Stitch Count: 27 × 29

315

367

Rose & Bow Pincushion
Stitch Count: 23 × 33

315

Position of pink ribbons

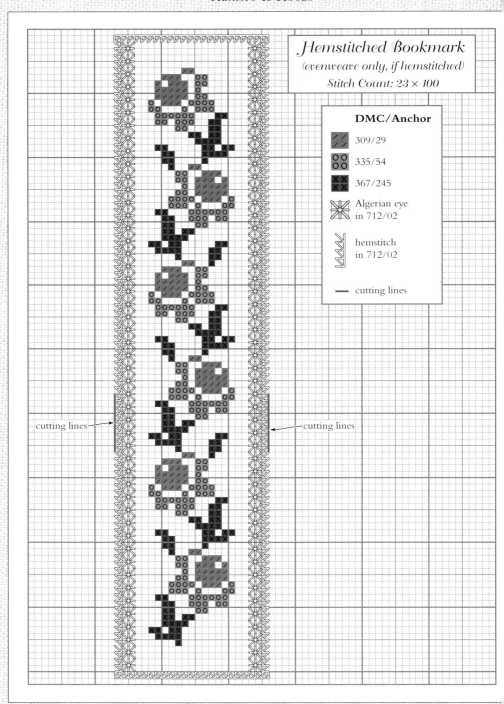

Hemstitched Bookmark
(evenweave only, if hemstitched)
Stitch Count: 23 × 100

DMC/Anchor

309/29

335/54

367/245

Algerian eye
in 712/02

hemstitch
in 712/02

— cutting lines

cutting lines →   ← cutting lines

Hearts & Roses

I have collected roses for years. The variety of colours, shapes and habits, and the wonderful heady scents, particularly from old-fashioned roses, make them my all-time favourites.

These designs make a set of needlework accessories, but you could use them for gift cards or trinket pots. The sampler (one of my most popular class projects) is not difficult: I'm sure you'll enjoy the various stitches used.

To work these projects refer to p 3, p 4 and stitch instructions on p 58. Refer to the charts on p 10–14 for thread requirements, stitch counts and specific stitch instructions. See p 52 for finishing instructions.

❋ Rose Band Sampler ❋

Design Size: 11×20 cm (4.25×8 in)
Fabric: 23×33 cm (9×13 in) 28-count Cashel linen (shade 101)
Also: Tapestry needle, size 22 for perlé

Work the bands as shown on the chart, leaving the hemstitching to the end. See p 62–3 for hemstitching instructions, and refer to the chart. Work two rows of hemstitch. Tie the vertical threads as shown on p 63.

❋ Rose Needlecase ❋

Design Size: 9×11.5 cm (3.5×4.5 in)
Fabric: 30.5×35.5 cm (12×14 in), 28-count Cashel linen (shade 101)
Also: 17.5×26 cm (7×10.25 in) Cashel linen for backing; two pieces white felt, each 18×9 cm (7×3.5 in), cut with pinking shears; 90 cm (36 in) antique-white cotton lace; 50 cm (19.5 in) 3 mm pink ribbon

Fold the fabric in half so the shorter sides meet and start stitching 1 cm (0.5 in) to the right of this fold – the unstitched half becomes the back of the needlecase. Work the Algerian eye stitches as shown on p 60, pulling slightly to form tiny central holes.

❋ Rose & Bow Pincushion ❋

Design Size: 4×6 cm (1.5×2.5 in)
Fabric: 15 cm (6 in) square 28-count Cashel linen (shade 101)
Also: 12.5 cm (5 in) square Cashel linen for backing; 50 cm (19.5 in) antique-white cotton lace; 50 cm (19.5 in) 3 mm pink ribbon; polyester filling;

❋ Rose Scissors Keeper ❋

Design Size: 5 cm square (2 in)
Fabric: 13 cm (5 in) square 28-count Cashel linen (shade 101)
Also: 9 cm (3.5 in) square Cashel linen for backing; 30 cm (12 in) antique-white cotton lace; 50 cm (19.5 in) 3 mm pink ribbon; polyester filling

❋ Hemstitched Bookmark ❋

Design Size: 4×18 cm (1.5×7 in)
Fabric: 7.5×33 cm (3×13 in) 28-count Cashel linen (shade 727)

To complete, hemstitch all edges (see p 62) to secure them. After hemstitching, trim the two long sides of the bookmark, then fray the remaining narrow ends.

(clockwise from top left)
Stitching Tote, Initial Needlecase,
Butterfly Picture, Fuchsia
Scissors Pocket

Fuchsias & Butterflies

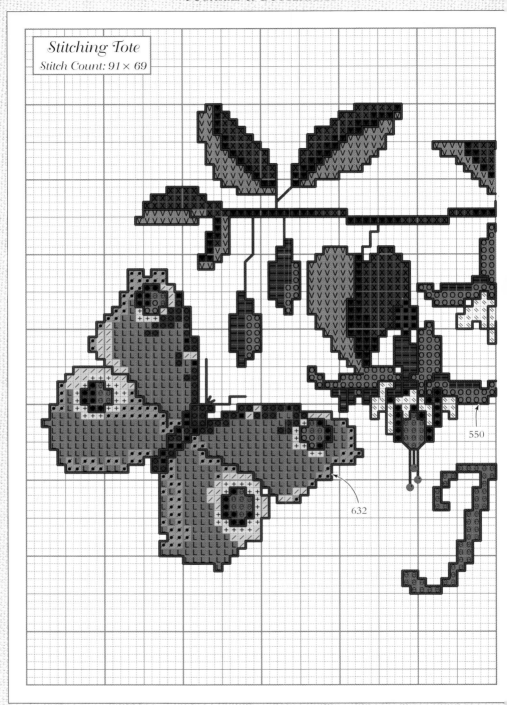

Stitching Tote
Stitch Count: 91 × 69

550

632

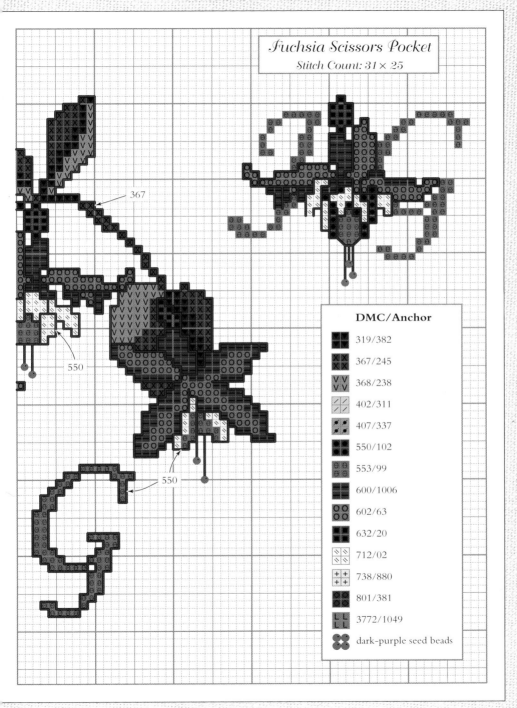

Fuchsia Scissors Pocket
Stitch Count: 31 × 25

367

550

550

550

	DMC/Anchor
	319/382
	367/245
	368/238
	402/311
	407/337
	550/102
	553/99
	600/1006
	602/63
	632/20
	712/02
	738/880
	801/381
	3772/1049
	dark-purple seed beads

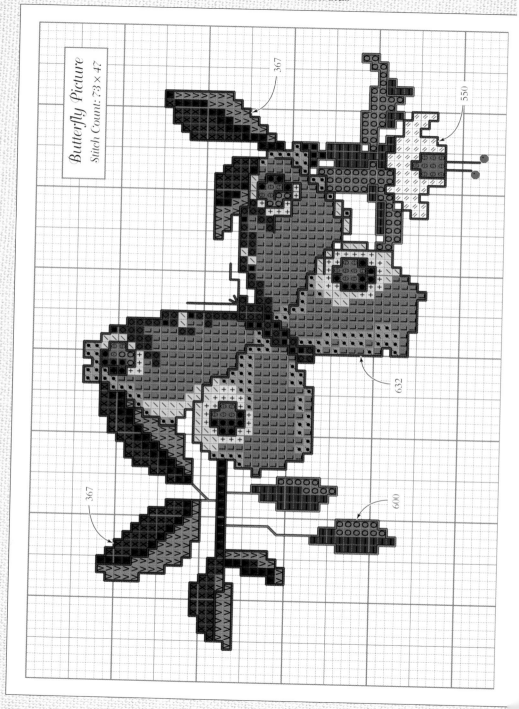

Butterfly Picture
Stitch Count: 73 × 47

367

550

632

367

600

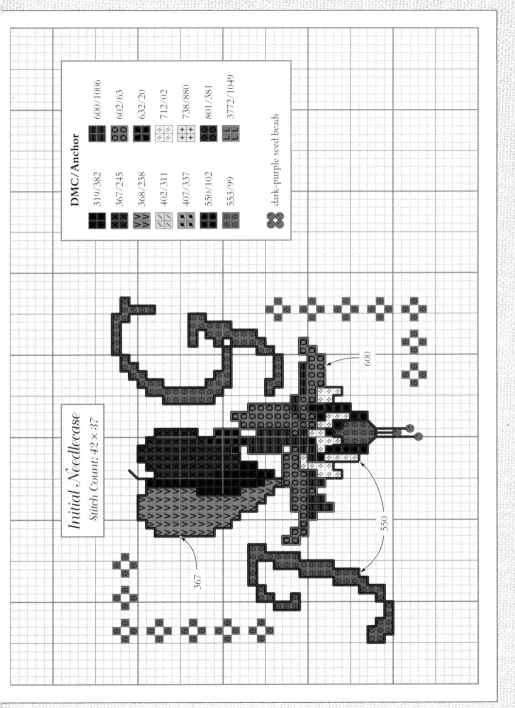

Initial Needlecase
Stitch Count: 42 × 37

DMC/Anchor

319/382	600/1006	
367/245	602/63	
368/238	632/20	
402/311	712/02	
407/337	738/880	
550/102	801/381	
553/99	3772/1049	
dark-purple seed beads		

600
550
367

Fuchsias & Butterflies

I try to encourage as many butterflies as possible to my garden – the peacock butterflies that cover our buddleia during the summer bring such joy. So it seemed only fair to include one of my favourites. I'm equally keen on fuchsias: this particular variety looks a little like a ballerina with frilly skirts!

In this section I have included more stitchers' treats such as the Stitching Tote – I can't be the only person who hates carrying her stitching in a plastic carrier bag!

The alphabet (with optional backstitch outline) is opposite. The beads are added (after the cross stitch is complete) using one strand of matching thread and a half cross stitch.

To work these projects refer also to p 3, p 4 and stitch instructions on p 58. Refer to the charts on p 18–21 for thread requirements, stitch counts and specific stitch instructions.

If you don't have a beading needle, use any needle that is fine enough to go through the holes in the beads.

To finish these projects, see p 52. You will need 70 cm (28 in) Liberty Tana Lawn fabric and wadding, and 3 m (3 yd) purple satin bias binding in total for all projects.

❋ Stitching Tote ❋

Design Size: 16.5×12.5 cm (6.5×5 in), stitched area only
Fabric: 29×33 cm (11.5×13 in) 28-count Cashel linen (shade 101)
Also: 7 dark-purple glass seed beads; beading needle; one piece 60×25 cm (23.5×10 in) and a second piece 41×25 cm (16×10 in) Liberty Tana Lawn fabric; 60×25 cm (23.5×10 in) polyester wadding; 1.40 m (55 in) purple satin bias binding

❋ Initial Needlecase ❋

Design Size: 7.5×7 cm (3×2.75 in)
Fabric: 18×17 cm (7×6.75 in) 28-count Cashel linen (shade 101)
Also: 3 dark-purple glass seed beads; beading needle; one piece 12×13 cm (4.75×5 in) and one piece 12×24 cm (4.75×9.5 in) Liberty Tana Lawn fabric; 12×24 cm (4.75×9.5 in) polyester wadding; two pieces of white felt 16×8 cm (6×3 in), cut with pinking shears; 80 cm (31.5 in) purple satin bias binding

❋ Fuchsia Scissors Pocket ❋

Design Size: 5.5×5 cm (2.25×2 in)
Fabric: 21.5×15 cm (8.5×6 in) 28-count Cashel linen (shade 101)
Also: 3 dark-purple glass seed beads; beading needle; one piece 24×12 cm (10×4.75 in) and three pieces 17×12 cm (6.75×4.75 in) Liberty Tana Lawn fabric; one piece 24×12 cm (10×4.75 in) and one piece 17×12 cm (6.75×4.75 in) polyester wadding; 70 cm (27.5 in) purple satin bias binding

❋ Butterfly Picture ❋

Design Size: 13×8 cm (5.25×3.25 in)
Fabric: 25×20 cm (10×8 in) 28-count Cashel linen (shade 101)
Also: 2 dark-purple glass seed beads; beading needle; purchased frame; polyester wadding

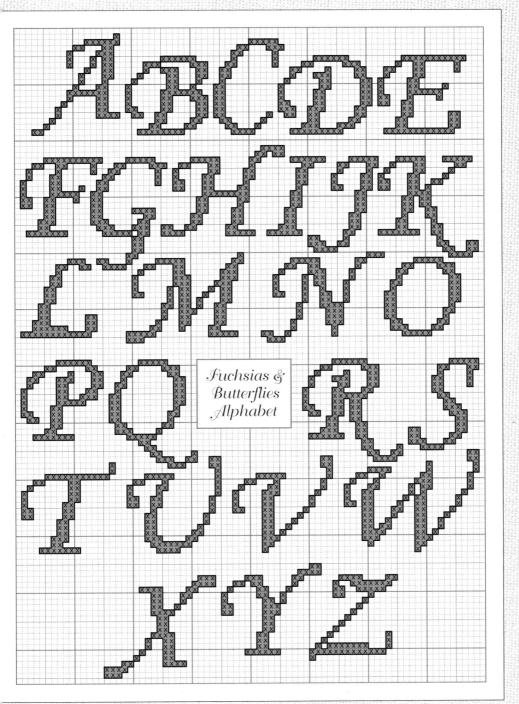

Fuchsias &
Butterflies
Alphabet

(clockwise from top left) Passion Flower Sampler, Wedding Ring Pillow, Bride's Token and Passion Flower Card

Passion Flowers

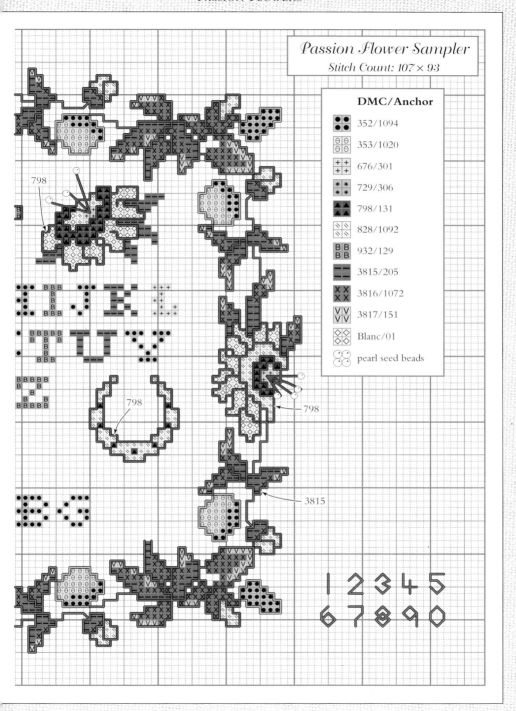

Passion Flower Sampler
Stitch Count: 107 × 93

DMC/Anchor

352/1094
353/1020
676/301
729/306
798/131
828/1092
932/129
3815/205
3816/1072
3817/151
Blanc/01
pearl seed beads

798

798

798

3815

3809

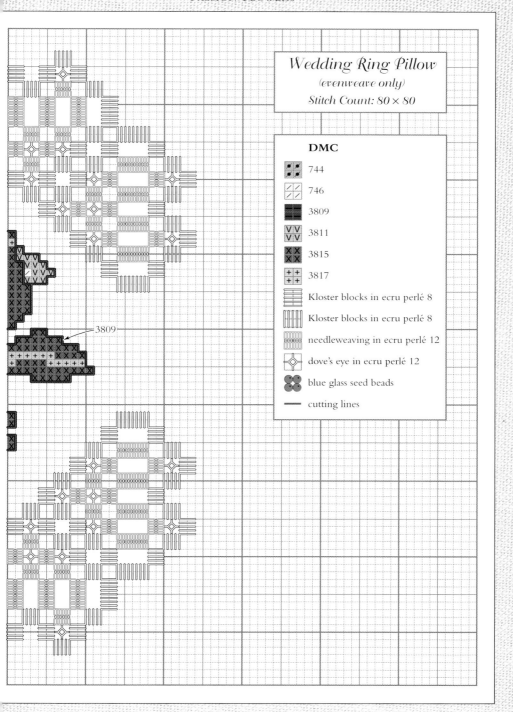

Wedding Ring Pillow
(evenweave only)
Stitch Count: 80 × 80

DMC

●● / ●●	744
╱╱ / ╱╱	746
▓▓	3809
VV / VV	3811
XX / XX	3815
++ / ++	3817
	Kloster blocks in ecru perlé 8
	Kloster blocks in ecru perlé 8
	needleweaving in ecru perlé 12
	dove's eye in ecru perlé 12
	blue glass seed beads
—	cutting lines

3809

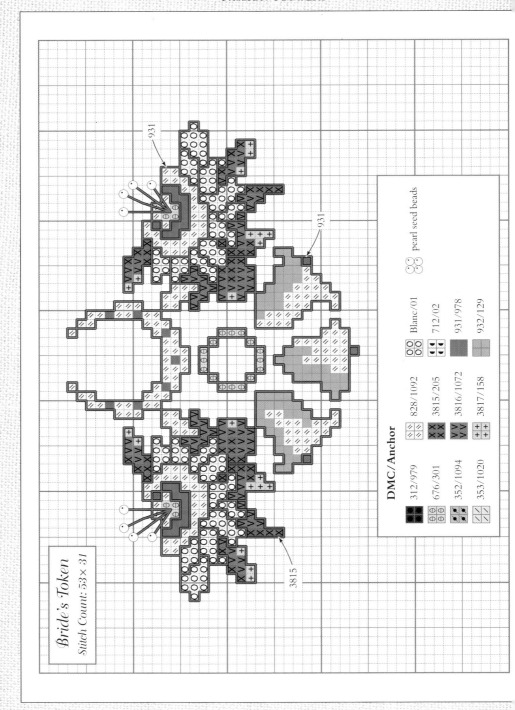

Bride's Token
Stitch Count: 53 × 31

DMC/Anchor

312/979	828/1092	Blanc/01	pearl seed beads
676/301	3815/205	712/02	
352/1094	3816/1072	931/978	
353/1020	3817/158	932/129	

Passion Flower Card
Stitch Count: 55 × 43

Passion Flowers

These amazing flowers have been a favourite since we discovered them in the garden at our very first house. Although passion flowers are often grown in conservatories, some varieties are hardy enough to grow outside. The flowers are so striking they can look quite unreal. I have included a pretty sampler and a bride's token in this section – something 'blue' for the bride to carry, perhaps.

The tiny glass beads on the stamens of the flowers could be replaced with French knots if preferred. (See p 59 for a foolproof version of the French knot.) If you don't have a beading needle, use any needle that is fine enough to go through the holes in the beads.

The Wedding Ring Pillow includes some basic Hardanger stitches, which give a beautiful, lacy effect, although they are very simple to stitch. (See p 61 for detailed instructions on Hardanger stitches: Kloster blocks, needleweaving and dove's eye.) The Wedding Ring Pillow is trimmed with a twisted cord and tassels, to complete the romantic feel.

To work these projects refer also to p 3, p 4 and stitch instructions on p 58. Refer to the charts on p 26–31 for thread requirements, stitch counts, specific stitch instructions, alphabet and numbers.

To finish the Sampler, Pillow and Token, see p 52. Note that you could make the cord and tassels for the Wedding Ring Pillow and Bride's Token out of the perlé thread used for the Hardanger. To finish the card (or make your own), see p 45.

✳ Wedding Ring Pillow ✳

Design Size: 14.5×14.5 cm (5.75×5.75 in)
Fabric: 27 cm (10.75 in) square 28-count Cashel linen (shade 101)
Also: 17 blue glass seed beads; beading needle; size 22 tapestry needle for perlé; two 21 cm (8.25 in) squares of pale aquamarine moiré satin; 70 cm (27.5 in) fine cream cord; four small cream tassels; polyester filling (enough to fill);

After the cross stitch is complete, work the Kloster blocks as shown on the chart on p 28–29 using one strand of perlé 8. Refer to the Hardanger diagrams on p 61.

Kloster blocks form the framework for the cut areas in Hardanger embroidery. They are formed with 5 vertical or horizontal straight stitches, each over 4 threads. The vertical and horizontal blocks meet at the corners, sharing the corner hole (this is vital). The secret of successful Hardanger is to count the Kloster blocks correctly. If they are in the right place the threads may be cut out and the stitching will not fall to pieces! The part-worked sample opposite shows how the Kloster blocks are worked and where to cut.

When all the Kloster blocks are complete (do not be tempted to cut any threads until the Kloster blocks are all stitched) cut the fabric threads as shown on the chart and in the part-worked sample opposite. The diagram shows that the threads are cut at the end of each block, never at the sides. When you have cut the threads and removed the loose ends you will have something like our sample.

Needleweave the threads between the Kloster blocks, adding the dove's eye as shown using one strand of perlé 12 (see p 61)

Add the optional beads to each flower stamen using one strand and a half cross stitch.

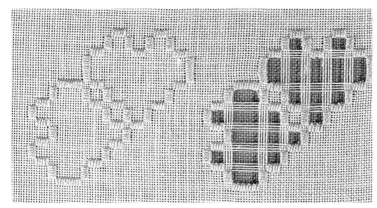

*Wedding Ring
Pillow: the Kloster
blocks for one of the
Hardanger corners,
shown stitched, then
with the fabric threads
cut. After cutting, the
loose threads were
removed to prepare for
the needleweaving*

✳ *Passion Flower Sampler* ✳

Design Size: 19×16.5 cm (7.5×6.5 in)
Fabric: 30.5×28 cm (12×11 in) 28–count
Cashel linen (shade 101)
Also: beading needle; 2 Goya or mother of
pearl bird buttons; 1 packet of pearl seed
beads; polyester wadding; purchased frame

After the cross stitch is complete, add beads to
each stamen using one strand of stranded cotton (floss) and a half cross stitch. Add buttons
using two strands of matching thread.

✳ *Bride's Token* ✳

Design Size: 10×5.5 cm (4×2.25 in)
Fabric: 20×16 cm (8×6.25 in) 28–count
Cashel linen (shade 101)
Also: 58 pearl seed beads for the stamens
and around the edges of the token; beading
needle; small piece stiff card; small piece
aquamarine satin moiré; small piece polyester wadding; 1 m (1 yd) cream 3 mm satin
ribbon and 1 m (1 yd) aquamarine 3 mm
satin ribbon, for handles and bows; small
cream tassel; double-sided adhesive tape

After the cross stitch is complete, add the
beads to each stamen using one strand of
stranded cotton (floss) and a half cross stitch.

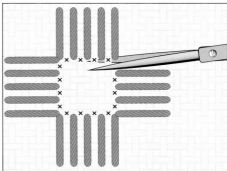

*Wedding Ring Pillow: cutting the Kloster blocks.
Work from a corner (a shared hole) and cut two
threads at a time, ensuring that you can see both
points of your scissors. The two squares shown
uncut at this stage (see above) could be left uncut
and filled with Algerian eye, if preferred*

✳ *Passion Flower Card* ✳

Design Size: 10×7.5 cm (4×3 in)
Fabric: 20×16 cm (8×6.5 in) 28–count
Cashel linen (shade 101)
Also: 16 pearl seed beads; beading needle;
purchased or home-made three-fold card
with 14.5×10 cm (5.75×4 in) oval aperture

After the cross stitch is complete, add the
beads to each stamen using one strand of
stranded cotton (floss) and a half cross stitch.

*(clockwise from top left)
Dragonfly Sampler and card.
Violet Sampler, violet card
and gift tags, Hardanger heart card*

Violas & Dragonflies

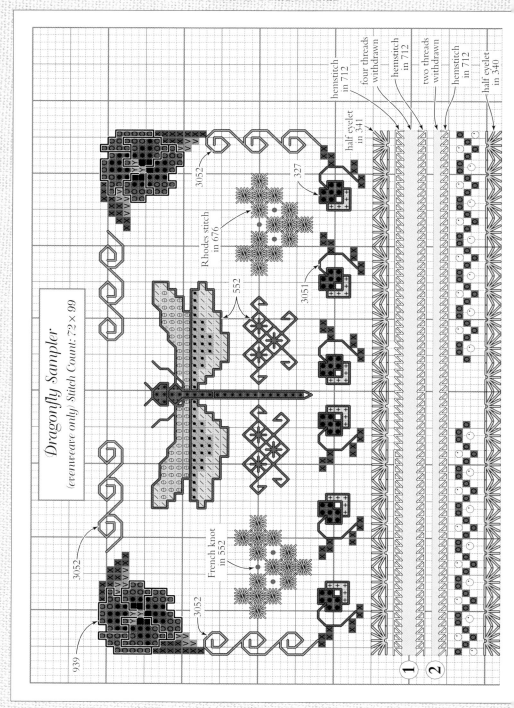

Dragonfly Sampler
(evenweave only) Stitch Count: 72 × 99

3052

Rhodes stitch
in 676

French knot
in 552

552

327

3051

half eyelet
in 341

hemstitch
in 712

four threads
withdrawn

hemstitch
in 712

two threads
withdrawn

hemstitch
in 712

half eyelet
in 340

3052

939

3052

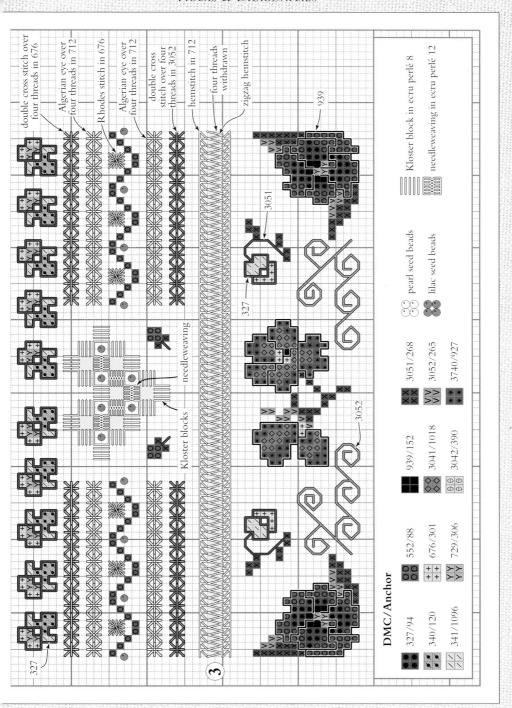

double cross stitch over four threads in 676

Algerian eye over four threads in 712

Rhodes stitch in 676

Algerian eye over four threads in 712

double cross stitch over four threads in 3052

hemstitch in 712

four threads withdrawn

zigzag hemstitch

Kloster block in ecru perlé 8

needleweaving in ecru perlé 12

pearl seed beads

lilac seed beads

939

3051

327

3052

needleweaving

Kloster blocks

DMC/Anchor

327/94	552/88	939/152	3051/268
340/120	676/301	3041/1018	3052/265
341/1096	729/306	3042/390	3740/927

327

③

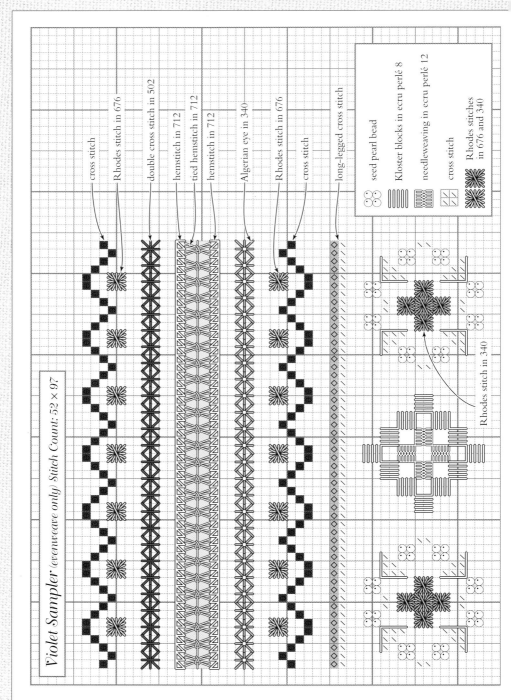

Violet Sampler (evenweave only) Stitch Count: 52 × 97

cross stitch

Rhodes stitch in 676

double cross stitch in 502

hemstitch in 712

tied hemstitch in 712

hemstitch in 712

Algerian eye in 340

Rhodes stitch in 676

cross stitch

long-legged cross stitch

seed pearl bead

Kloster blocks in ecru perlé 8

needleweaving in ecru perlé 12

cross stitch

Rhodes stitches in 676 and 340

Rhodes stitch in 340

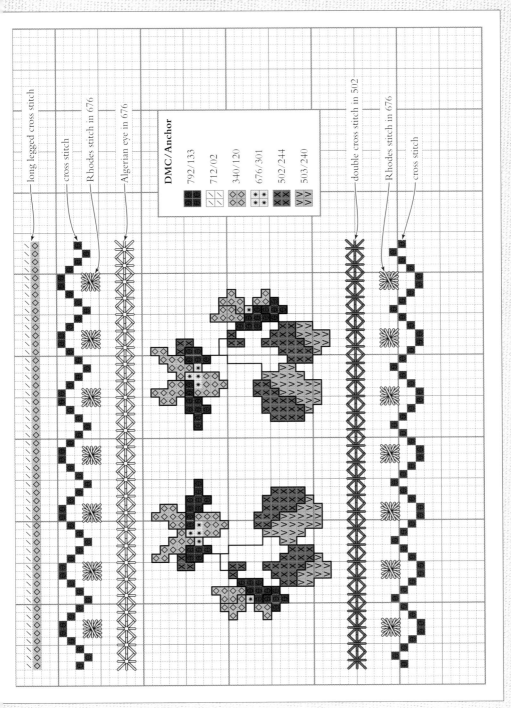

long legged cross stitch

cross stitch

Rhodes stitch in 676

Algerian eye in 676

DMC/Anchor

792/133
712/02
340/120
676/301
502/244
503/240

double cross stitch in 502

Rhodes stitch in 676

cross stitch

Violas & Dragonflies

Pansies and violets, their smiling faces turned towards the sun, are some of the sweetest flowers. And, with today's selection of winter flowering plants on offer, we can enjoy these lovely flowers all year around. I have included a delicate dragonfly among the violas because dragonflies are so attractive and simple to stitch, and because they were often included in traditional band samplers.

Both samplers in this section include small amounts of Hardanger and various counted stitches as well as cross stitch. (See p 61 for detailed instructions on Hardanger stitches: Kloster blocks, needleweaving and dove's eye.)

Work a row of tacking threads to mark the centre of the sampler and to act as an early warning system if you miscount.

Avoid coming up through occupied holes (where a stitch has already been formed); instead, wherever possible, insert the needle from the front. This prevents spoiling existing perfect stitches.

Try to avoid running out of thread halfway across the band. If you should do so, stitch and park the short end (see p 7), start the new thread using an away waste knot (p 58) and work a few stitches, then finish the short end in the direction you are stitching.

If you don't have a beading needle, use any needle that is fine enough to go through the holes in the beads.

To work these projects refer also to p 3, p 4 and stitch instructions on p 58. Refer to p 7 for additional guidelines for working band samplers. Refer to the charts on p 36–9 for thread requirements, stitch counts and specific stitch instructions.

❊ Dragonfly Sampler ❊

This exquisite little band sampler is one of my personal favourites because, although small, it is packed with interesting stitches and techniques. This makes it perfect for enhancing your stitching skills.

You may have noticed that this design is not quite symmetrical. This is because, to combine Hardanger with those interesting counted thread stitches and the dragonfly motif, I had to 'compensate' somewhere. Because there is an odd number of fabric threads in the dragonfly body, it will not 'square up' with the central Hardanger motif. A useful tip when charting in such a situation is to lose the extra stitch somewhere away from the the centre if you can. This helps to create the illusion that both sides match.

Design Size: 12.5×18 cm (5×7 in)
Fabric: 25.5×30.5 cm (10×12 in) 28-count Cashel linen (shade 101)
Also: beading needle; size 22 tapestry needle for perlé; 26 pearl seed beads; 14 violet glass seed beads

Start the design by counting to the row of small viola heads worked in cross stitch and one strand of outlining. Note that this band starts and finishes two threads in from the edge of the other bands. Work from the centre of this band and then work all other bands from the left hand side following your tacking guidelines (see p 7). From this point you can count up or down, referring to the chart for details of technique and thread.

Work the dragonfly wings in one strand of stranded cotton (floss) in half cross stitch.

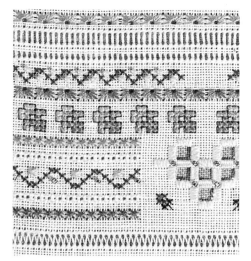

Detail of the Dragonfly Sampler, showing the various counted stitches, including hemstitch

For the hemstitch bands, threads are withdrawn and re-woven in to the side of each band to create a 'selvage'. To do this, carefully snip horizontal threads in the centre of the band and, using a needle, unpick these to the edge of the design. Then either completely remove each alternate thread and weave one of the unravelled threads in its place, or re-weave all the cut threads in to the existing fabric. I have used the latter method which, although simple, does mean that you can see the re-woven area more clearly. You will be left with vertical fabric threads that may be hemstitched as zig-zags as in band 3 or left plain as in bands 1 and 2 (see p 62–3).

For the Hardanger section, refer to the Hardanger diagrams on p 61. When all the Kloster blocks are complete (do not be tempted to cut any threads until all blocks are stitched) cut the fabric threads (see p 33). Needleweave the remaining threads using one strand of perlé 12.

The beads are added after all the other stitching is complete, using matching threads and a half cross stitch.

❊ *Violet Sampler* ❊

This sampler is very pretty but less complex than the Dragonfly Sampler. The beads are part of the counted design, so they could be replaced by cross stitch (this is not possible in the Dragonfly Sampler).

Design Size: 9.5×17 cm (3.75×6.75 in) excluding optional hemmed edge
Fabric: 20×28 cm (8×11 in) 28-count Cashel linen (shade 101)
Also: Beading needle; size 22 tapestry needle for perlé; 64 pearl seed beads

Refer to the chart for detailed instructions on each band, leaving the hemstitch bands and Hardanger section in the centre until the end.

After the cross stitch is complete, work the Kloster blocks as shown on the chart on p 38-9 using one strand of perlé 8. Refer to Hardanger instructions on p 61. When all the Kloster blocks are complete (do not be tempted to cut any threads until the Kloster blocks are all stitched) cut the fabric threads as shown on the chart. Needleweave the remaining threads as shown on p 61, using one strand of perlé 12.

Add the beads after the cross stitch is complete, using matching threads and a half cross stitch. Our sampler has an optional hemstitch border – instructions are on p 62.

❊ *Gift Cards* ❊

I have worked some of the small motifs from these charts on Cashel linen to make little gift cards – always useful for special occasions. They are mounted in three-fold cards (see Suppliers and p 45).

The dragonfly card is worked in perfect cross stitch in two strands. The Hardanger heart motif is on unbleached linen and mounted in a hand-cut card. The two gift tags are stitched on coloured fabric, and the violet card is stitched on cream linen.

(clockwise from top left)
Geranium Card on
pale-green fabric, Rosebud Card,
Nasturtium Card, Daisy Card,
Rose Card, Sweet Pea Card, Poppy Card
and Geranium Card on pink fabric

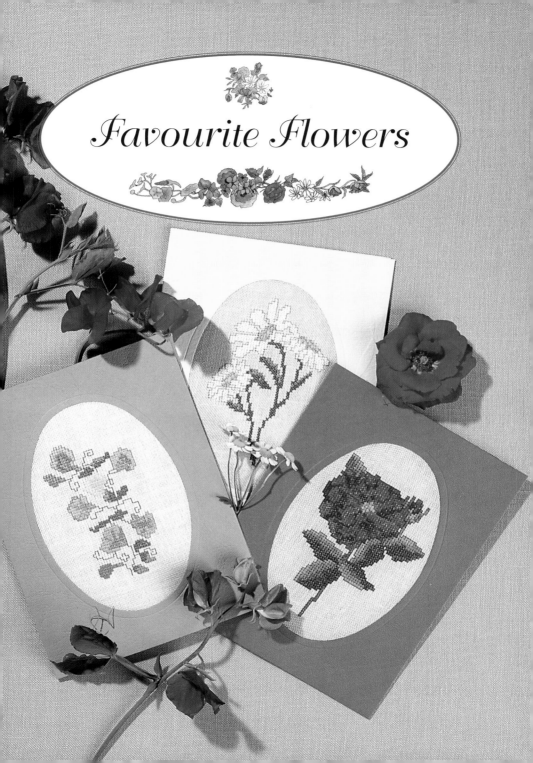

Favourite Flowers

Favourite Flowers

This personal selection of favourite flowers gives interesting but simple gift card ideas in pure cross stitch and backstitch (see p 42–3) on 28-count Cashel linen. If personalised with lettering, they can be used for many different occasions. When combined, they make a delicious stitched sampler (see p 46–7).

To stitch a card, work your chosen flower from the chart positioning it centrally on the fabric, bearing in mind the aperture of your card. The details below give a fabric quantity for each flower and a card aperture to fit, if worked on 28-count Cashel linen. Mount your stitched flowers in purchased or home-made, three-fold cards, or mount and frame them as a set of small pictures.

I have worked the geranium on two different coloured fabrics, to show how this can change the effect of a design, and to encourage you to be adventurous with fabric.

To work these projects refer also to p 3, p 4 and stitch instructions on p 58. Refer to the charts on p 48–51 for thread requirements and stitch counts.

If you use a different count fabric which would make the designs smaller or larger you will need to calculate your fabric requirements (see opposite).

❋ Geranium Card ❋

Design Size: 11×11.5cm (4.25×4.5in)
Fabric: 20×20cm (8×8in) pink/pale-green
Card aperture: 14cm (5.5in) diameter

❋ Nasturtium Card ❋

Design Size: 9×6cm (3.5×2.5in)
Fabric: 16×14cm (6.5×5.5in) antique-white
Card aperture: 9×6.5cm (3.5×2.5in)

❋ Sweet Pea Card ❋

Design Size: 6×10cm (2.5×4in)
Fabric: 20×16cm (8×6.5in) cream
Card aperture: 14.5×10cm (5.75×4in) oval

❋ Poppy Card ❋

Design Size: 6×7.5cm (2.5×3in)
Fabric: 18×12cm (7×4.75in) pale-blue
Card aperture: 10.5×8cm (4.25×3.25in) oval

❋ Rose Card ❋

Design Size: 9×11.5cm (3.25×4.5in)
Fabric: 20×16cm (8×6.5in) ecru
Card aperture: 14.5×10cm (5.75×4in) oval

❋ Daisy Card ❋

Design Size: 7.5×11.5cm (3×4.5in)
Fabric: 20×16cm (8×6.5in) ecru
Card aperture: 14.5×10cm (5.75×4in) oval

❋ Rosebud Card ❋

Design Size: 4 cm square (1.5in)
Fabric: 18×12cm (7×4.75in) white
Card aperture: 10.5×8cm (4.25×3.25in) oval

Making and mounting cards

It is often difficult to find the right size and colour of card, so, why not try making your own? Always pad them, unless very small. Buy thin wadding or the card may distort – if it seems too thick, just pull off a layer.

You will need:

Cutting mat; sharp craft knife (small, with a good point); set square; metal ruler; pencil; sheet of coloured card (Canford card is easy to cut, with a good selection of colours); thin polyester wadding; adhesive or double-sided tape; gold or silver pen (one that draws fine lines without blotting)

1. Plan the size of aperture, then the card (bottom margin wider than top and sides).

2. Draw the card, on the wrong side, using the set square for corners. Draw three sections, the aperture in the middle. Pressing down firmly on the ruler and cutting slowly along it, cut the card, then the aperture. Rectangular apertures are easy to cut this way. The hand-cut circular and oval apertures in this book were cut using the rims of cups, glasses and small oval dishes as templates.

3. Score the two fold lines on the inside by running the back of the knife along the ruler. Fold the card, and check all edges meet. If necessary, trim the inner section, and edges. Add lines and embellishments.

4. Press your finished stitching carefully on the wrong side on several layers of towel.

5. If using padding, cut a piece of polyester wadding the same size as the aperture.

6. Open the card. Check the design fits the aperture. Trim the fabric to same size as the card. Apply a thin coat of adhesive or double-sided tape to the inside of the aperture. Lay the stitching face up and place the aperture over it. Check the position before pressing it down. Lay the pre-cut wadding over the back of the stitching, exactly behind the aperture. Put a dab of adhesive or a short length of tape in the centre of the fold-in section. Fold this

section in to stick on the wadding and hold it exactly behind your stitching.

7. Secure the fold-in section with adhesive or tape. If your finished card seems a little buckled when completely dry, press it under a pile of books, protecting the stitching with wadding to prevent it being crushed.

Calculating fabric requirements

Calculating fabric requirements is something that many stitchers avoid, but it is not difficult and it gives much greater freedom in the fabrics you use and the projects you make. Any project can be adapted to make a smaller or larger design, on a finer or coarser fabric. When you make any quantity of cards, you will want to use a variety of card mounts (or, make your own). If you have a card with a specific size aperture, you can choose a fabric that will make your design fit that aperture.

All counted cross stitch designs are made up of squares or parts of squares, and the fabrics used have the same number of threads (or blocks) in each direction so that you will produce nice square stitches. The number of these fabric threads per inch/2.5 cm (the thread count of the fabric, e.g. 28-count) and the stitch count of a design (the number of stitches by height and width) determine the finished size of the stitched design.

To calculate a design size in inches on an evenweave fabric (including linen) where you are stitching over two threads: divide the stitch count of the design (in each direction) by half the thread count of the fabric (14, in the case of 28-count linen). Thus, the Geranium Card has a stitch count of 59×62; which gives $59 \div 14 = 4.2$; and $62 \div 14 = 4.4$. Rounded up, this gives a design size of 4.25×4.5 in (11×11.5 cm).

To calculate a design size in inches on an evenweave fabric (including linen) where you are stitching over one thread: divide the stitch count by the thread count.

To calculate a design size on aida, divide the stitch count by the thread count.

✳ *Favourite Flowers Sampler* ✳

This pretty sampler is a combination of all the flower charts in this section, stitched on a gorgeous blue-and-white checked fabric called Gomera. The fabric is evenweave, and the check pattern is used as a random background, but it could be incorporated as part of a design. I have frayed the edges of my sampler, but you may prefer to mount and frame your version.

To recreate this design or one very similar I recommend that you draw a layout chart. This is very simple. Copy the outline of each flower on to a piece of squared paper and then cut out each one. Using another piece of squared paper, arrange the flower motifs until you are satisfied with the result and then stick them in position. Stitch each flower from the charts on p 48–51, using your layout chart to check their position.

Refer also to p 3, p 4 and stitch instructions on p 58. Refer to the charts on p 48–51 for thread requirements and stitch counts.

The stitch count and design size below are for the design shown but your version may vary.

Stitch Count: 119×133
Design Size: 21.5×24 cm (8.5×9.5 in)
Fabric: 33×35.5 cm (13×14 in) 28-count Zweigart blue-checked Gomera fabric (available from the Cross Stitch Guild)

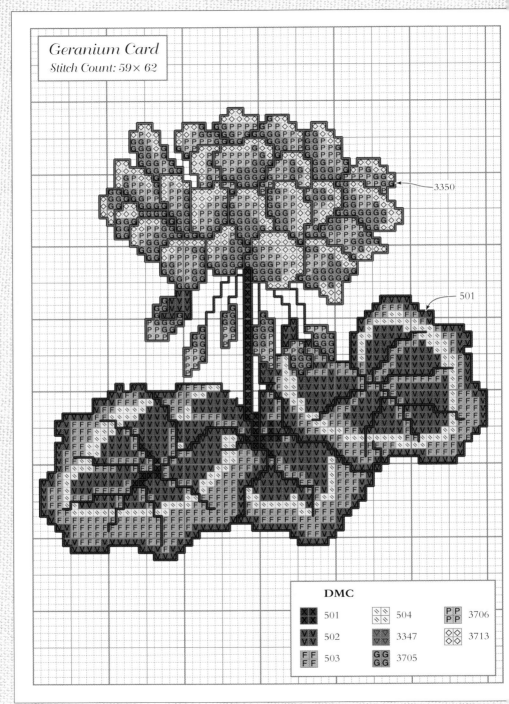

Geranium Card
Stitch Count: 59 × 62

3350

501

DMC

✕✕	501	◇◇	504	P P / P P	3706
V V	502	▽▽	3347	◇◇	3713
F F / F F	503	G G / G G	3705		

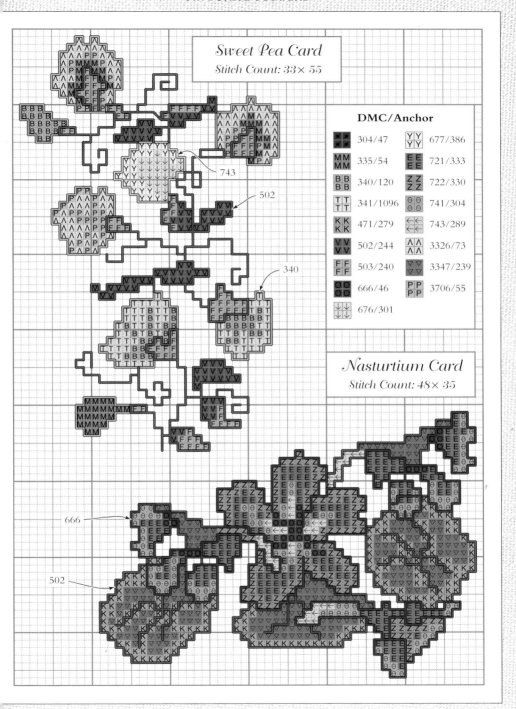

Sweet Pea Card
Stitch Count: 33× 55

DMC/Anchor

▦	304/47	Y Y	677/386
MM	335/54	E E	721/333
B B	340/120	Z Z	722/330
T T	341/1096	θ θ	741/304
K K	471/279	← ←	743/289
V V	502/244	∧ ∧	3326/73
F F	503/240	▽ ▽	3347/239
O O	666/46	P P	3706/55
↓ ↓	676/301		

743

502

340

Nasturtium Card
Stitch Count: 48× 35

666

502

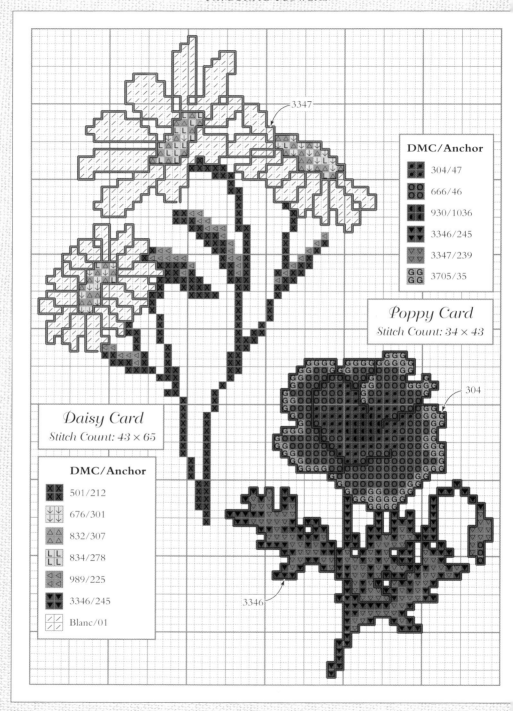

3347

DMC/Anchor

304/47	
666/46	
930/1036	
3346/245	
3347/239	
3705/35	

Poppy Card
Stitch Count: 34 × 43

304

Daisy Card
Stitch Count: 43 × 65

DMC/Anchor

501/212	
676/301	
832/307	
834/278	
989/225	
3346/245	
Blanc/01	

3346

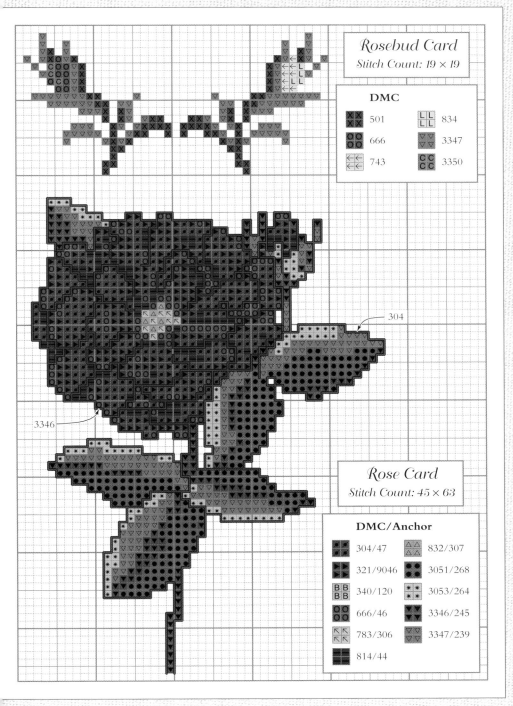

Rosebud Card
Stitch Count: 19 × 19

DMC

▓▓	501	L L / L L	834
O O	666	▽▽	3347
←←	743	C C / C C	3350

304

3346

Rose Card
Stitch Count: 45 × 63

DMC/Anchor

304/47		832/307	
321/9046		3051/268	
340/120		3053/264	
666/46		3346/245	
783/306		3347/239	
814/44			

Finishing the Projects

The finishing instructions which follow are for the hand-finished projects in this book, such as the needlecases, pincushions, and scissors keepers. The materials needed are listed on the relevant project pages (see individual page references given below).

In this small book there is not space to give full instructions for stretching, framing and mounting, but this information is given in detail in my book *The Cross Stitcher's Bible* (David & Charles), or for Cross Stitch Guild members, in back issues of *News & Views*.

❋ Rose Needlecase ❋
(see p 8–15)

1. Press your embroidery carefully on the wrong side. Fold in half to find the needlecase spine, 1 cm (0.5 in) to the left of the stitching. Trim both layers to within 3 cm (1.25 in) of the embroidery on the other three sides.

2. Stitch the lace 2 cm (1.75 in) in from the edge, right sides together, finished lace edge inwards, gathering as you go.

3. Lay the backing linen on the embroidered linen, right sides together and stitch a 2 cm (1.75 in) seam round all edges, leaving an opening for turning. Take care not to catch the edges of the lace in this seam.

4. Trim the seam, clip the corners and turn right sides out. Slipstitch the opening. Press again to sharpen the edges.

5. Fold the two pieces of felt in half and stitch them to the spine to make the pages of the needlecase.

6. Tie the ribbon around the spine to trim.

❋ Rose & Bow Pincushion ❋
(see p 8–15)

1. Stitch ribbons round the design as marked on the chart. Trim the embroidery to a 12.5 cm (5 in) square, centring the design on the fabric.

2. Stitch the lace 2 cm (1.75 in) in from the edge, right sides together, finished lace edge inwards, gathering as you go.

3. Lay the backing linen on the embroidered linen, right sides together and stitch a 2 cm (1.75 in) seam round all edges, leaving an opening for turning. Take care not to catch the edges of the lace in this seam.

4. Trim the seam, clip the corners and turn right sides out. Fill with polyester filling and slipstitch the opening.

❋ Rose Scissors Keeper ❋
(see p 8–15)

1. Press your embroidery carefully on the wrong side. Trim the embroidery to a 9 cm (3.5 in) square, centring the design.

2. Stitch the lace 2 cm (1.75 in) in from the edge, right sides together, finished lace edge inwards, gathering as you go.

3. Add a ribbon loop to one corner.

4. Lay the backing linen on the embroidered linen, right sides together and stitch a 2 cm (1.75 in) seam round all edges, leaving an opening for turning. Take care not to catch the edges of the lace or the ribbon loop in this seam.

5. Trim the seam, clip the corners and turn right sides out. Fill with polyester filling and slipstitch the opening.

❋ Stitching Tote ❋
(see p 16–23)

1. Press your embroidery carefully on the wrong side and trim to 21×25 cm (7×9 in). Making a 1 cm (0.5 in) seam, attach the embroidery to one end of the shorter piece of Tana Lawn.

2. Lay the larger piece of Tana Lawn right side down and cover with the wadding. Place the first piece of Lawn (with the embroidery attached) on top, right side up. Line up all edges carefully and stitch the layers together around these edges.

3. Make a line of stitches through all layers at the seam where the embroidery meets the Lawn. Make a second line 20 cm (8 in) away from the first line, in the centre of the Tana Lawn. This divides the whole into three equal sections and makes 'hinges' to enable your tote to fold well along the stitched lines.

4. Bind the end that is not the embroidery.

5. Fold the Tana Lawn section to make the pocket of the tote. Stitch the sides together.

6. Trim the corners of the embroidered section (the flap) into curves. (Draw around a cup as a guide.)

7. Bind from one bottom corner up one side, around the flap, and down the other side.

✳ Fuchsia Scissors Pocket ✳
(see p 16–23)

1. Make templates by tracing the two pattern pieces onto fairly stiff card.

2. Press your embroidery carefully on the wrong side and trim to 12×9 cm (4.75×3.5 in).

3. Taking a 1 cm (0.5 in) seam, attach the embroidery to the shorter side of one of the three smaller pieces of Tana Lawn.

4. Using a pencil, draw the round the back and flap template (overleaf) on to the larger piece of Tana Lawn. Then draw round the pocket front template (overleaf) onto each of the two smaller pieces of Tana Lawn.

5. Lay the larger piece of Tana Lawn right side down, and cover with the larger piece of wadding. Place the piece of Tana Lawn with the embroidery attached on top, right side up. Line up all pieces, with the embroidery in the centre of the flap. Stitch around the pencil lines. Then trim very close to the stitched line to give you the right shape for the back of the scissors pocket. (This is a much easier method than cutting the individual shapes first and then trying to line up small pieces of fabric and wadding.)

6. Repeat this 'wadding sandwich' method

with the two smaller pieces of Tana Lawn and the remaining piece of wadding, to make the front of the scissors pocket. Bind the top edge of the pocket front.

7. Place the front on the back. Stitch the edges to hold in place. Trim all edges, then bind, making a neat join at the bottom.

✳ Initial Needlecase ✳
(see p 16–23)

1. Press your embroidery carefully on the wrong side and trim to 13×12 cm (5×4.75 in): the 13 cm (5 in) measurement is the width of the needlecase, plus an extra 1 cm (0.5 in) seam allowance which should be positioned to the left of the design.

2. Place the embroidery right sides together with the smaller piece of Tana Lawn and sew a 1 cm (0.5 in) seam on the right side .

3. Lay the larger piece of Tana Lawn right side down, cover with the wadding, then the seamed pieces, right sides up. Align all edges carefully and stitch together around these edges. Stitch through all layers at the seam where the embroidery meets the Tana Lawn to make the spine of the needlecase.

4. Bind all round the edge, making a neat join at the bottom.

✳ Wedding Ring Pillow ✳
(see p 24–33)

1. Press your embroidery carefully on the wrong side and trim the fabric to a 21 cm (8.25 in) square.

2. Lay one piece of moiré right side up, lay the embroidery, also right side up, over it, then lay the second square of moiré right side down. Stitch a 2 cm (0.75 in) seam round all edges, leaving an opening for turning.

3. Trim the seam, clip the corners and turn right sides out. Fill with polyester filling and slipstitch the opening.

4. Attach a tassel to each corner and slipstitch the cord around the edges of the pillow (over the seam), tucking the two ends into the slipstitching to finish.

❋ *Bride's Token* ❋
(see p 24–33)

1. Press your embroidery carefully on the wrong side. Trace the pattern onto fairly stiff card. Cover the card with wadding, secured with double-sided tape and trimmed to exactly the same shape as the card.

2. Lay the embroidery over the wadded card. Pin into the edges of the card, stretching the embroidery over the shape. Pin tightly and carefully so that the design is central and well stretched. When the embroidery is straight and secure trim away the excess fabric, leaving a 4 cm (1.5 in) border.

3. Apply double-sided tape to the back of the card. Pull the excess fabric over to the back of the card and stick it down. This is fiddly, so work bit by bit and clip the curves so that they can open up to be secured.

4. Attach the tassel to the back of the bottom edge.

5. Cover the back with satin moiré, trimming, clipping and turning in the edges to fit. Slipstitch all round the edge.

6. Sew seed beads at regular intervals all round the edge.

7. Attach the ribbons to the top points, adding loops to trim.

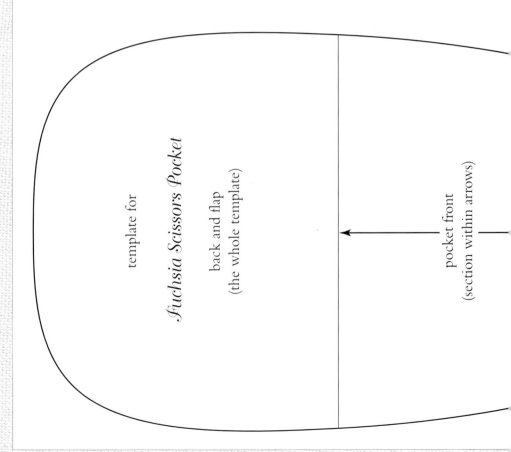

template for

Fuchsia Scissors Pocket

back and flap
(the whole template)

pocket front
(section within arrows)

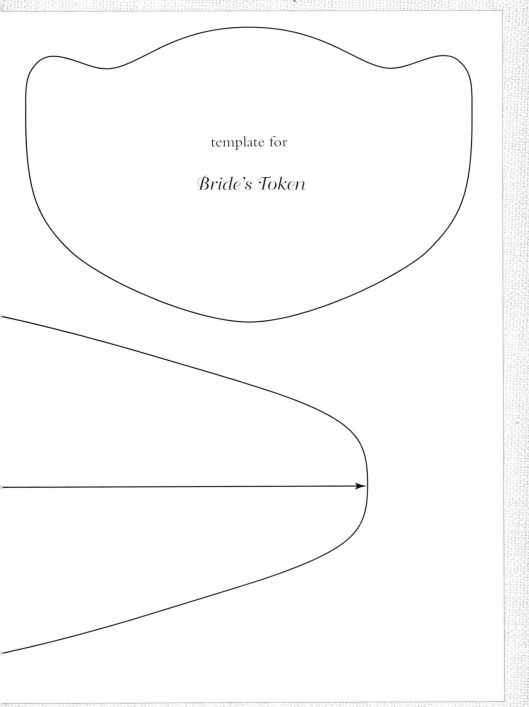

template for

Bride's Token

Stitches

All the stitches needed for the projects in this book can be found in the following pages. See also p 4 and p 6–7 for cross stitch on linen, and perfect cross stitching.

I have created the Heart Stitch Sampler shown on this page to show the potential of the stitches. It is worked on a Zweigart ready-hemmed heart (originally designed for table-cloths), which is available from the Cross Stitch Guild. This design does not have a chart but I have selected stitches and motifs contained within this book so that you can reproduce it as shown here, or create your own version. The rose motif comes from the chart on p 14, and the bands are all made up of stitches included in the next few pages, plus somersault hemstitch below.

When working a design on an unusual shape it is vital to work centre tacking (basting) lines and count very carefully.

I have added tiny mother of pearl buttons but you may prefer to add a charm or replace some of the cross stitch with beads. Seed beads are perfect for 28-count fabric – any larger and the fabric may distort as the beads crowd on top of one another. When selecting metal charms, avoid cheap brass or stamped versions as they can eventually discolour your fabric. Use only good-quality charms as they will have been 'scoured' to prevent damage.

Somersault hemstitch

Follow the instructions on p 63 for tied hem-stitch, but take the needle over four threads. Reverse the needle, place it under two threads then over two, then twist the needle the other way. This will twist the fabric threads automatically. Pinch your fingers over the threads, and gently pull the needle through, keeping the thread horizontal and taut. Repeat down the row, fastening off into the fabric edge.

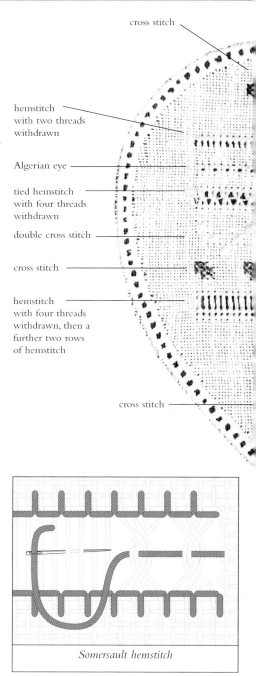

cross stitch

hemstitch with two threads withdrawn

Algerian eye

tied hemstitch with four threads withdrawn

double cross stitch

cross stitch

hemstitch with four threads withdrawn, then a further two rows of hemstitch

cross stitch

Somersault hemstitch

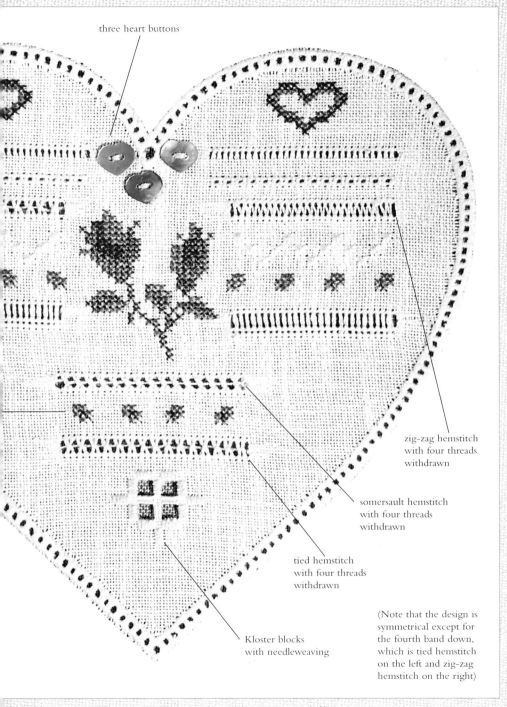

three heart buttons

zig-zag hemstitch
with four threads
withdrawn

somersault hemstitch
with four threads
withdrawn

tied hemstitch
with four threads
withdrawn

Kloster blocks
with needleweaving

(Note that the design is
symmetrical except for
the fourth band down,
which is tied hemstitch
on the left and zig-zag
hemstitch on the right)

Knotless loop start

This method only works if you are stitching with an even number of strands, i.e. 2, 4, or 6 strands. Cut the stranded cotton (floss) into lengths roughly twice as long as you would normally use, and carefully separate one strand (or 2, or 3).

Double this strand and thread your needle with the two ends together. Pierce your fabric from the wrong side where you intend to place the first stitch, leaving the looped end at the back. Make the first stitch, taking the needle through to the back and passing it through the loop. The stitch and thread are now anchored. (See also p 4 and p 6)

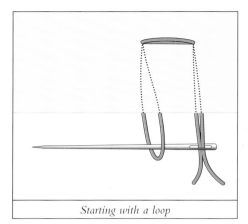

Starting with a loop

Away waste knot start

The away waste knot is useful when you are using an odd number of strands, or when you are mixing threads in the needle (such as when 'tweeding' threads to achieve a mottled tweedy appearance). You would also use it if you were following the guidelines for perfect cross stitch and realigning the threads before starting to stitch (see p 6).

Leave the knot on the front of the fabric, along the 'route' you are going to stitch. Work towards the knot, then cut it off when the threads are anchored. Avoid using this method with black thread, which may leave a shadow on the fabric. (See also p 4 and p 6)

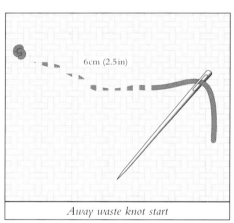

6cm (2.5in)

Away waste knot start

Finishing / changing thread

There are two ways of making a neat finish. The first way is to pass the needle under stitches of the same or a similar colour at the back of the work, and snip off the loose end close to the stitching.

Or, to prevent any distortion of stitches on the front of the fabric (which can happen with the first method), finish the thread in the direction of the stitching. To do this, park the needle above the design. Thread a new needle with replacement thread and work a few stitches. Un-park the needle and finish the old thread under the new stitches.

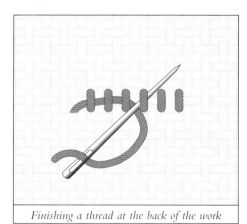

Finishing a thread at the back of the work

Backstitch

Backstitch is used for creating an outline around a design, or part of a design, to add detail or emphasis. On a chart, it is usually indicated by solid lines surrounding the symbols. It is always added after the cross stitch has been completed, to prevent the backstitch line being broken by the cross stitch.

Outlining with backstitch is not always necessary, and is often a matter of taste. Avoid black for outlining, unless needed specifically for the design. Use colours that enhance, rather than overpower. Work over pairs of threads on evenweave, avoiding long stitches unless specified for details.

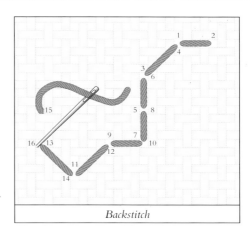

Backstitch

French knot

Bring the needle through to the front of the fabric, wind the thread around the needle twice and 'post' the needle partly through to the back, one thread or part of a block away from the entry point. (This stops the stitch pulling to the wrong side.) Gently pull the thread you have wound so that it sits snugly at the point where the needle enters the fabric. Pull the needle through to the back and you should have a perfect knot in position.

If you want bigger knots, add more thread to the needle – this gives a much better finish than winding the thread more times round the needle.

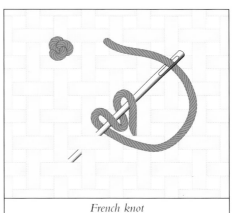

French knot

Rhodes stitch

Rhodes stitch gives a solid, slightly raised, effect, like a series of 'studs'. It is particularly successful when worked in thread which has a sheen, to emphasise areas of light and shade.

Each stitch is worked over squares of two, four or more threads of evenweave fabric. (Rhodes stitch does not work well on aida.)

As the stitch is built up, working in an anticlockwise direction around the square, the centre becomes raised. Follow the sequence of stitching carefully, as shown. Maintain the same sequence for every stitch to achieve a uniform effect throughout.

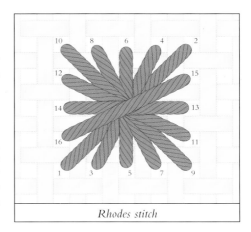

Rhodes stitch

Double cross stitch

Double cross stitch is worked over four or two threads of an evenweave fabric, or over four blocks of aida, to create a series of bold crosses or 'stars'.

Work a normal cross stitch first, then add a vertical cross on top. To keep all double cross stitches uniform, make sure the direction of the stitches within them is the same. The second cross can be worked in a different colour to add interest, in which case work the stitch in two stages: all the lower crosses first, followed by the top crosses.

Also known as Smyrna or leviathan stitch.

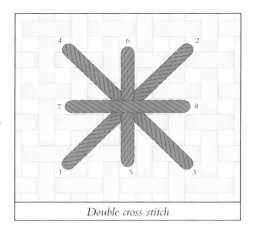

Double cross stitch

Algerian eye

This pretty star-shaped stitch usually occupies the space taken by four cross stitches. It is worked in such a way that a small hole is formed in the centre (pull quite firmly). Working from left to right, work round each stitch in an anticlockwise direction, or vice versa. Algerian eye can be worked over one or two threads as shown.

The secret for perfecting Algerian eye is to always work the stitch by passing the needle down through the central hole, as shown in the diagram, and to take care that trailing threads do not cover this hole as you progress to the next stitch.

Also known as star stitch and eyelet stitch.

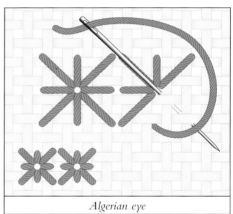

Algerian eye

Long-legged cross stitch

Long-legged cross stitch gives a plaited-braid effect which is often used for borders and for joining edges to make a seam. It also looks impressive when worked in rows.

To work this stitch on evenweave, move four threads forwards and two threads upwards in a long diagonal 'leg', then work two threads downwards followed by two threads backwards diagonally to make the short leg. Long-legged cross stitch can also be worked on aida.

Also known as long-armed Slav stitch, and Portuguese stitch.

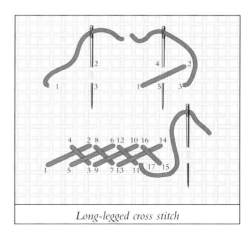

Long-legged cross stitch

Hardanger: Kloster blocks

Kloster blocks form the framework for the cut areas in Hardanger. They are formed with 5 vertical or 5 horizontal straight stitches, each of them over 4 threads on evenweave. Hardanger is usually worked in perlé.

Work the stitches side by side so that they look the same on the wrong side. Vertical and horizontal blocks meet at the corners, sharing the corner hole (this is vital). Check that you have counted correctly and that the blocks are opposite one another. Then there will be no problems when you cut the threads at the next stage. Cut the threads at the end of the Kloster blocks, never at the side (see p 33).

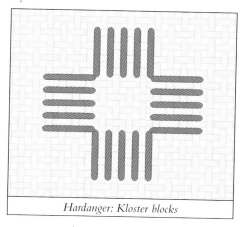

Hardanger: Kloster blocks

Hardanger: needleweaving

Needleweaving is used on the loose threads that are left when Kloster blocks have been cut (see above and p 33). It creates covered bars, and the spaces left between these can be filled with decorative stitches such as dove's eye filling (see below). Use a slightly finer thread than for the Kloster blocks.

To weave a bar, pass the needle down through the centre of the loose threads and work over and under pairs of threads as shown. After completing one bar, weave the next one at right angles to it, working around the design, taking care not to run threads across the back of the cut areas.

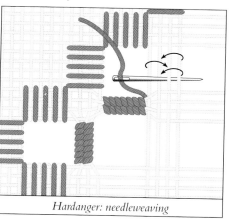

Hardanger: needleweaving

Hardanger: dove's eye filling

Dove's eye can be added after needleweaving, but it is best worked at the same time (see above). Whilst needleweaving the last side of a square, work to the centre of the bar, then bring the needle out through the central void. Pierce the neighbouring Kloster block or needlewoven bar halfway along its length, bringing the needle up through the void and through the loop formed by the thread. Continue around the square, following the diagram, but before resuming the needleweaving, loop the needle under the first stitch to form the final twist in the dove's eye.

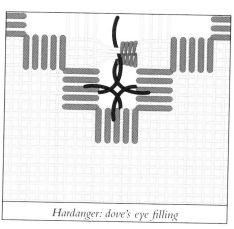

Hardanger: dove's eye filling

Hemstitch (evenweave only)

Hemstitch is a versatile stitch allowing you to hem a raw edge (as in the Hemstitched Bookmark, p 14), form a folded hem (as in the Violet Sampler, p 34) or remove horizontal threads from the fabric leaving the vertical threads to be decorated (as in the Dragonfly Sampler, p 34).

HEMSTITCHING A RAW EDGE

Work a straight stitch across two threads, turning the needle to face horizontally. Make another straight stitch at right angles to the first, then pass the needle diagonally under two threads. Repeat the straight stitches along the row, counting carefully. After the hemstitching is complete, the threads indicated may be cut away.

HEMSTITCHING A FOLDED HEM

Count out 10 fabric threads from the stitching on all edges and mark these positions with pins. On each side, cut the tenth (marked) fabric thread at its centre, unweave the cut thread back to the corners and re-weave back in to the fabric (diagram 1).

Score the fabric so you can make straight folds without pressing. Count out 9 threads from the missing one on each side, lay the fabric on a hard surface and place the blunt end of a fairly large tapestry needle (22–20) in the groove between threads 9 and 10. Pull the fabric under the needle (rather than the needle over the fabric), pressing firmly on the needle and pulling hard. Repeat to make another line a further 9 threads out. The linen now makes a straight fold at the scorings (washing is necessary to remove these folds).

Count out another 7 threads and cut very carefully between threads 7 and 8 (diagram 2). Handle the linen carefully from now on to prevent fraying.

Fold in the corners and cut as shown in diagram 3. Fold in all the edges and you will find that the corners are mitred. Pin or tack the hem in place. Hemstitch all sides (diagram 4). As you come to the corners, close the mitres with a few invisible stitches.

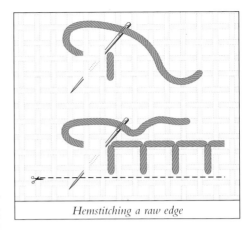

Hemstitching a raw edge

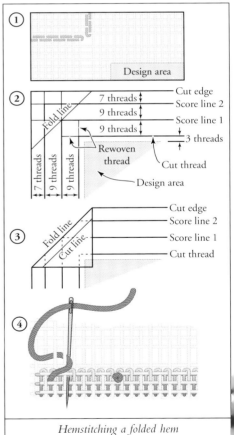

Hemstitching a folded hem

Hemstitch with horizontal threads removed

When hemstitch is worked in rows, the horizontal fabric threads between the rows can be removed, leaving the vertical fabric threads. These can be left plain as in the Dragonfly Sampler (see p 41), or they can be used as the framework for a number of decorative filling stitches, such as tied hemstitch or zig-zag hemstitch (also used in the Dragonfly Sampler).

To stitch the hemstitch rows, follow the diagram for hemstitching a raw edge (left), but cut the horizontal threads between the two rows, and re-weave them into the fabric (see p 41), rather than trimming the fabric.

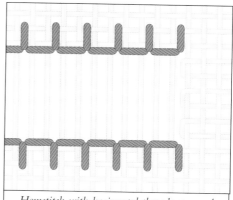
Hemstitch with horizontal threads removed

Tied hemstitch

This simple hemstitch variation is created by first hemstitching two rows and withdrawing the intervening horizontal threads (see p 41). The number of withdrawn threads will depend on the chart you are following. Then use the needle to tie groups of four threads together. Start with an away waste knot, bringing the needle up at the side of the row of vertical threads, midway between the two rows of hemstitch. Take the needle over four fabric threads, make a loop, take the needle round the back of the four threads, then up through the loop to make a knot. Keep the knotted line as straight as possible.

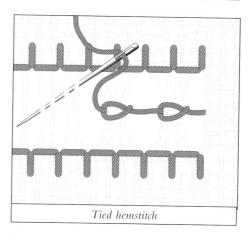
Tied hemstitch

Zig-zag hemstitch

To make zig-zag hemstitch, stitch one row of hemstitch. Stitch over two threads of fabric as above, or over four threads as shown here. Then stitch a second row above or below the first, but starting one thread further in (fill the gap with a short stitch). As you stitch, the zig-zag effect will appear.

Zig-zag hemstitch is used to create a row in the Dragonfly Sampler (see p 41).

Another variation, somersault hemstitch, is used in the Heart Stitch Sampler (see p 56–7). For further hemstitch variations, see *The Cross Stitcher's Bible* (David & Charles).

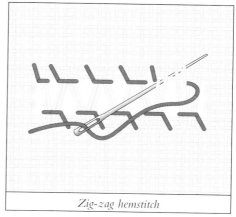
Zig-zag hemstitch

Acknowledgements

It is not possible for an author to complete a project like this without the help and support of a special team. My heartfelt thanks go to all of the people mentioned below.

Sue Hawkins (CSG Technical Editor) for supervising the technical and making up sections and completing the projects with her usual expertise. Vivienne Wells, our esteemed editor, who has project managed this book from start to finish, has kept me in order, on time and was always right! Ethan Danielson for excellent charts and diagrams. Brenda Morrison for designing the pages and the gorgeous cover. Pete Canning, for the superb photography. Sarah Jane Gillespie for giving me the idea and providing the exquisite flower paintings.

Rainer Steimann of Zweigart & Sawitzki for encouragement and supplies. Len and Malcolm Turner of Fabric Flair for fabric and beads. DMC Creative World and Coats Crafts UK for their generous supplies of stranded cotton (floss) and perlé.

My brilliant team of stitchers and pattern checkers: Barbara Webster, Sue Moir, Lesley Clegg, Michelle Edwards, Barbara Grenville, Sue Smith, Mary Miles, Deborah Buglass, Jean Fox, Michelle Daniels, Jill Vaughan, Hanne Fentiman, Sue Bridgens, Su Maddocks, Margaret Pallant, and Janet Jarvis.

Suppliers

Card Art for three-fold cards
14, Kensington Industrial Park, Hall Street, Southport PR9 0NY
Tel: +44 (0) 174 549754

Fabric Flair for supplies of Interstitch Minster and seed beads
Northlands Industrial Estate, Copheap Lane, Warminster, Wilts BA12 0BG
Tel: +44 (0) 1985 846845

DMC Creative World Ltd
(Suppliers of Zweigart fabrics, UK)
Pullman Road, Wigston,
Leics LE18 2DY
Tel: +44 (0) 1162 811040

Zweigart, Joan Toggitt Ltd
(Suppliers of Zweigart fabrics, USA, Canada)
262 Old New Brunswick Road, Unit E,
Piscataway, NJ 08854–3756, USA
Tel: +1 732 562 8888

Zweigart & Sawitzki (Suppliers of Zweigart fabrics in all other countries)
PO Box 120, 71043 Sindelfingen, Germany
Tel: +49 (0) 7031 7955

The Cross Stitch Guild (see below) for fabric hearts and Gomera fabric

Liberty of London for Liberty Tana Lawn and cotton lace
Regent Street, London W1R 6AH
Tel: +44 (0) 207 734 1234

Jane Greenoff's Inglestone Collection for gold-plated needles, stitch catchers, etc
Yells Yard, Cirencester Road, Fairford, Glos GL7 4AR
Tel: +44 (0) 1285 712778

The Cross Stitch Guild

Members of the Cross Stitch Guild (founded 1996) receive a bi-monthly colour magazine, with designs, technical advice and information, news, competitions and giveaways, plus discounts at CSG Retail Partner Shops and on CSG Weekends. You will soon be able to contact us via the CSG website, featuring the Stitcher's Market and Inglestone Collection catalogue. For further information contact:
The Cross Stitch Guild
Freefone (UK only): 0800 328 9750
Tel: +44 (0) 1285 713678
email: *greenoff@easynet.co.uk*
www.thecrossstitchguild.com